TO TELL THE TRUTH
BASIC QUESTIONS AND BEST
EXPLANATIONS

J. ANDREW KIRK

The Latimer Trust

The Latimer Trust (formerly Latimer House, Oxford) is a conservative Evangelical research organisation within the Church of England, whose main aim is to promote the history and theology of Anglicanism as understood by those in the Reformed tradition. Interested readers are welcome to consult its website for further details of its many activities.

The Latimer Trust
London N14 4PS UK
Registered Charity: 1084337
Company Number: 4104465
Web: www.latimertrust.org
E-mail: administrator@latimertrust.org

Refreshingly clear, admirably concise, and humbly confident, Andrew Kirk's robust biblical response to secular accounts of the origins and meaning of life and how to live it well is a brilliant example of the adage that if you want to explain something simply, you need to understand it profoundly. Importantly, despite the book's brevity, Andrew Kirk takes great care to represent rival explanations fairly and to avoid caricature. As such, this is a wonderful resource for anyone looking to understand for themselves, and explain to others, why and how Christianity provides a uniquely rational, coherent and satisfying explanation of the meaning of human existence. At the same time, Kirk's encouragement is not just to tell the truth but to demonstrate it through lives that have been and are being transformed by the grace of the creator redeemer God who has provided his Son to enable human beings to live in the freedom and fullness they yearn for. Highly recommended.

Mark Greene
Mission Champion
Executive Director LICC

In the midst of a cultural and political war on truth and pervasive moral relativism, Andrew Kirk's clear exposure of the explanatory inadequacy and incoherence of atheist and humanist views will be a most helpful resource for those who still have opportunities to argue for the truth and power of the biblical Christian worldview. Kirk is equally clear, however, that such truth not only shapes our thinking but must also transform our living.

Revd Dr Christopher J. H. Wright
Langham Partnership
Author of *The God I Don't Understand* (Zondervan)

This is an excellent introduction to Christian apologetics, providing an accessible overview of the great themes of the nature of truth, purpose, human identity, and the reality of good and evil. Here is a winsome commendation of Christian theism combined with an insightful exposure of the emptiness of modern secularism, all earthed in a call for

Christian living which demonstrates the reconciling power of the gospel. Each chapter concludes with questions for reflection which will be especially appreciated by those using this study [book] for group study.

Revd Canon Charles Raven
GAFCON

This book is a cogent, bare hands approach to issues raised by western secular societies sceptical of the truth claims of the Christian faith. It is a compelling apologia for modern materialists who think that above us is only sky, and a virtual catechism for post-modern people baffled by the immensities of nature, the mystery of life and death, of who we are and what the world is about.

Melba Padilla Maggay, PhD
President of the Institute for Studies in Asian Church and Culture (ISACC)

A really helpful introduction to apologetics, this short book takes us carefully and logically through the big questions about truth, human value, good and evil, and how to live rightly in a broken world. Ethics is not just philosophy, but a wonderful opportunity to point people to our good, true and beautiful saviour, Jesus.

Dr Giles Cattermole
London Team Leader for UCCF: The Christian Unions and a Consultant in Emergency Medicine

CONTENTS

FOREWORD

Andrew Kirk is a distinguished mission theologian and practitioner. Here, once again, in this little book, he shows evidence of wide reading and analytical skills. He is asking in the book how we can give a good account of our faith with gentleness and respect. Such an exercise has usually been called 'apologetics', though Andrew prefers the term 'advocacy'.

For him, Christian faith is simply the best explanation for the big questions about the meaning of life, human destiny and the origin and purpose of the Universe. We cannot justify notions of human dignity, equality, and liberty without invoking transcendental principles, best supplied by the Bible's teaching that we are all made in God's image and destined for intimate friendship with him. Moral awareness is innate in human beings and there is no reason why it should arise in a universe brought about by mere chance and evolution which is blind.

The empirical sciences, as far as they go, can describe phenomena and the relationship between them. But description is not explanation. For explanation, we need another order of discourse which is about purpose, love, creation and redemption.

Christianity produces Jesus as God's revelation of his love and his purpose not only to create but to redeem what has gone badly wrong. He is also the normative person who shows what it is to be authentically human.

'Secular' values are often parasitic on the Judaeo- Christian tradition of the Bible. Secularism promotes values it cannot ground in and justify from a wider narrative. Persons as moral agents, freedom and responsibility, conscience and knowing right from wrong all demand an explanation, as does the physical and living Universe.

We are indebted to Andrew for such effective advocacy of a Christian world view.
Bishop Michael Nazir-Ali
OXTRAD: Oxford Centre for Training, Research, Advocacy & Dialogue

PREFACE

There are two main motives for this brief book. Firstly, I wish to try and set the record straight about central aspects of the Christian faith, given the considerable misunderstanding displayed by otherwise intelligent commentators in the Western world concerning the rational basis for its beliefs. Secondly, I would like to be able to offer Christians credible reasons for being able to claim that their convictions about life provide the best explanations for the meaning and realities of human existence. Its intention is to examine the core beliefs and practices of Christian faith in the light of the most basic questions that confront every generation.

Reflecting the overall title of the book, the first question asks: What is truth and how can it be known? This introductory chapter explains the purpose and fruitfulness of justifying the truth of Christian convictions about God, the universe, life on earth and human experience in all its diversity (often called 'apologetics'). The nature of truth and how one may discover it is, perhaps, the most fundamental issue that challenges human thought in every age.

The second question asks: Why are we humans here and who are we? The chapter explores various explanations about the origins of the universe, life on planet earth and the human species. It considers both belief in the creation of everything by a personal divine being and the alternatives proposed by those who do not believe there is a God. It draws out the implications of both views in the quest for human identity.

The third question asks: Why does life embody both good and evil? In this chapter, I explore the reasons why humans can be both considerate and compassionate, but also corrupt and culpable. I examine the nature of goodness and evil – and look at possible origins of evil. I compare the answers given by both Christian and secular belief systems to account for this dual reality and discuss the reasons why a Christian worldview gives a more convincing explanation.

The fourth question asks: How may evil be overcome, and goodness promoted? The material in this chapter focuses on the Christian story of how God enters human history to end the destructive forces of evil in human relationships and to create a new way of being human. I will compare the Christian view with other explanations of how society should view defective human nature.

The fifth and final question asks: How then should we live? Here, I look at the Christian conviction that the best way to live has been shown by the one whom Christians believe has created the whole of reality and, particularly, men and women in his image. I will then begin by exploring the provision that God has made for the good life. At the same time, I will compare and contrast these with other ideas about how ethical values can be substantiated and should be implemented.

The material covered is limited. Much more can be said on all sides for each of the questions raised. The discussion undertaken here is indicative of the kind of answers or explanations which the Christian faith is capable of giving to the most basic issues with which human beings have to grapple. Indeed, it is part of the uniqueness of human experience that these questions continue to demand plausible responses. These vary enormously according to the basic presuppositions that different people bring to the discussion.

In societies where secular beliefs and values have come to predominate in public debate and in their educational systems, it is not easy to engage creatively with the big questions from a Christian perspective. All too often, the conversation seems to founder on misunderstandings and misinterpretations. This is particularly true concerning the nature of reason and faith and the part that each plays in producing and supporting basic convictions about the meaning of existence and how it should be lived.

The idea that faith in a God – who is said to have revealed himself and his will to the world through specially chosen messengers – must be irrational is repeated time and again. That it constitutes an illusory 'leap in the dark' has almost become a secular dogma which no amount of sane, coherent discussion is able to dislodge. The appallingly ignorant interpretations given of Christian beliefs by some atheistic scientists, philosophers and other commentators who undertake to air publicly their opinions about religious matters, are compelling witnesses to this reality. Ignorance is excusable in certain circumstances. However, when the same errors are trotted out over and over again, despite the record having been put straight in numerous books, articles, blogs and public debates, there is no justification for repeating the same inaccuracies and distortions.

3

This book may not be able to persuade the detractors of Christian faith to portray its beliefs accurately. Nevertheless, it may prove useful in showing Christians why and how their fundamental convictions can be defended rationally – namely, on the basis of substantial evidence and sound arguments. If it helps to clarify some of the most contentious debates in contemporary societies and enables Christians to speak with confidence about their convictions in the face of ridicule and misrepresentation, it will have fulfilled a purpose.

The questions at the end of each chapter are intended to stimulate reflection and discussion. If, as the Christian faith emphatically maintains, its beliefs are reasonable, accord with reality and can be defended on the basis of solid, well-informed arguments, then Christians are duty-bound to think intelligently about their commitments. It is part of their calling that Christians challenge the false assumptions on which secular, humanistic creeds are based – at every opportunity and in every walk of life. False doctrines lead to false conclusions about the reality of human living. Ultimately, they are destructive of human well-being.

Following from the discussion so far, it is probably obvious that the context I have in mind for the reflections of this book is the underlying worldview of secularist, Western societies. For the sake of brevity, I have not attempted to mount a dialogue with non-Christian religions. Such an endeavour would require a much longer discussion. This book is intended to be as concise as possible, given the elaborate nature of the themes presented. I hope, nevertheless, that members of other faiths, especially those living in societies influenced by current secular, humanistic beliefs, will find this contribution to the discovery of truth about human reality constructive and beneficial.

Just one word of caution: Christians should be robust in debate, but never contentious or disputatious for the sake of winning arguments. The whole point of indicating the explanatory power of the Christian message to identify truth about the whole of life is to encourage people to become followers of Jesus – the way, the truth and the life. It behoves Christians, therefore, to avoid at all costs any semblance of arrogance which points to their own wisdom or cleverness. Reasoned advocacy of one's beliefs is persuasive to the degree that it is undertaken with genuine humility and an unpretentious disposition.

Witness to the truth is properly carried out by listening to others, respecting their full humanity and entering their world of ideas and opinions, however much we may disagree with them. It means making every effort to enter into conversations based on the recognition of the other person's equal worth. Self-effacing human to human contact is the finest way of sharing one's core convictions and allowing other people to share theirs.

J. Andrew Kirk

February 2020

1. Knowing the Truth: Existence as it is

Introduction

The defence and promotion of the truth of the Christian faith has been given the title of 'apologetics', within the academic discipline of theology. The word is derived from a well-known verse in the New Testament: 'Always be ready to make your defence to anyone who demands from you an account of the hope that is in you' (1 Peter 3:15). Some translations use the word 'answer' in place of 'defence'. The English word translates the Greek word *apologia* – hence, apologetics.[1]

Unfortunately, in modern English the word is associated more with apologising. This is not the intended meaning. Indeed, it is the very opposite of what Paul calls 'the confirmation of the gospel' (Philippians 1:7). Advocacy, on the other hand, has a more positive ring about it. An advocate is one who defends or promotes a cause. It is used, for example, of lawyers who act either as prosecutors or defenders in a court of law.

Christianity has always seen advocacy as one of its missionary tasks. The so-called 'Apologists' of the second century, for example, defended their faith against accusations of atheism, cannibalism and incest – atheism because they would not subscribe to the deity of the Roman emperor, cannibalism because they talked about eating the body and drinking the blood of Jesus Christ, and incest because they married those they called 'brothers' and 'sisters'. They also aimed to present Christian thought in a favourable light, arguing for its truth and demonstrating how absurd and contradictory were alternative interpretations of the reality and meaning of human life.

The task has not changed much today. The contemporary world bears a number of resemblances to that of the Roman empire in the first and second centuries. Christianity in Western nations is, in terms of the number of people who practise it seriously, again a minority religion. It is often misrepresented in the media and elsewhere in the public arena.

---

[1] The word is also used in Acts 22:1; 1 Corinthians 9:3; Philippians 1:7 and 2 Timothy 4:16.

It is disliked and vilified, mainly because it insists that human well-being depends on acknowledging the authority of God, revealed in Jesus, over the whole of life. Christian believers, therefore, cannot endorse lax moral standards, just because they spring from a social consensus about what is acceptable or unacceptable behaviour.

So, Christians are constrained to clarify what they do, and do not, believe – and why they claim that the Christian faith is a true account of the real world. The most adequate reason for becoming a Christian and renouncing alternative religious or secular beliefs is that Christianity is true and other worldviews are wrong at their core.[2]

Misunderstandings of Christian belief

Too often non-Christians writing about the Christian faith distort its true meaning. Almost every day one can find examples in the press. The authors of leading articles and opinions simply have not done their homework properly. They continue to repeat misguided ideas that have long since been refuted. Let me take just one example to illustrate the point.

Oliver Kamm, a columnist for *The Times Newspaper*, reflecting on a speech made by Ian McEwan (novelist and author of *Atonement*) at the Oxford Literary Festival wrote an article entitled, 'Secular values, not religion, make us a tolerant society':

---

[2] An understanding of the meaning of secular is complex. I am using it in this book principally of the following beliefs: there is no final reality beyond the universe; the basis of all existing entities is material; the right use of reason is the only means of knowing all that can be known; religious convictions and practices should be excluded from the public arena; moral judgements arise from the nature and experience of human life, without recourse to a divine being; religion is not needed to enjoy a profound quality of life. I explore the meaning of secular in more detail in my books, *The Church and the World: Understanding the Relevance of Mission* (Milton Keynes: Paternoster Press, 2014), Chapter 12, and in *Being Human: An Historical Inquiry Into Who We Are* (Eugene, OR: Wipf and Stock, 2019), Chapter 10.

Religious belief resolves no moral problem and yields no knowledge ... Religions have a lethal assumption in common: that faith is a virtue.[3]

Each of the three assertions in these two short sentences are wrong. They are all based on the tacit, fallacious assumptions that only scientific research can produce knowledge and solve ethical dilemmas and that faith is based on wishful thinking, without any evidence to back it up. He was commenting on a phrase that McEwan had emphasised in his talk, that 'the secular mind is better equipped than religion to reach reasoned and compassionate judgements.'

Kamm does not state whether McEwan produced any evidence for his bald declaration. As a matter of fact, there is plenty of evidence that can be adduced to refute the allegation. McEwan published a novel in September 2014 called *The Children Act*. It is about a fictitious couple who refuse medical treatment for their child. It should not surprise anyone that the couple are designated as members of the Jehovah's Witnesses. One presumes that McEwan has taken this non-Christian sect as a typical example of religion, just so that he can denounce its inhumane treatment, on religious grounds, of a life-saving blood-transfusion.

These two representative, secular humanist writers are asserting that religious claims are incompatible with proper rational thought, that faith and reason are irreconcilable and that, therefore, faith has to be eliminated in order for people to be able to think straight. Another claim that is being made is that a secular view of life is morally superior to a Christian one. In the course of this book, I will argue the exact opposite, giving a number of examples of why secular convictions, if followed consistently, are not particularly rational.

Science and evidence

It is crucial to realise that secular convictions, contrary to the belief of many secularists, are not based on reason alone or on science alone. Science itself is based on a number of assumptions that cannot be demonstrated by the methods that science is entitled to use as it

---

[3]   Oliver Kamm, 'Secular values, not religion, make us a tolerant society', *The Times*, 5 April 2014.

investigates aspects of the world and the universe. One of these premises is that material substance is the most basic reality of all existence. This is not a conclusion derived from purely empirical, experimental investigation. It is a prior presumption taken into the scientific enterprise as a speculative conjecture. It has itself become *an article of faith* that has the ability to distort scientific findings.

Science explores a reality that is already given. It uncovers mechanisms that are there and presumed to be constant. Around three-quarters of the original founding members of the Royal Society (founded in 1660) were devout Christian believers; many of them were theologians as well as practising scientists. They believed that there are two basic, non-contradictory sources of knowledge – the *world*, to be explored by means of scientific research, and the *word* of God, to be explored through a proper interpretation of the Bible.

The main accusation levelled against the Christian faith by non-religious believers is that it is not based on evidence, and therefore there are no adequate reasons for believing that its claims to know the truth are valid. If this allegation were true, the secularist would be right to suspend belief. However, as we will aim to show, there is plenty of evidence – from observing the world around us, from scientific theories (especially in the fields of cosmology and biology), from history, philosophical thinking and moral judgements – to make a highly plausible case for Christian faith. It is not the lack of evidence that is the problem. Rather, people who think this way are looking in the wrong place, for they have far too narrow a view of what counts as plausible evidence.

Contrary to the views of Oliver Kamm, Ian McEwan, Richard Dawkins, the Humanist Association and countless other sceptics, faith is not 'belief, in spite of, or even because of lack of evidence'.[4] They are simply plain wrong to assert that 'faith is not allowed to justify itself by argument.'[5] Sadly, these people display wilful (because their views have been shown countless times to be false) ignorance. Indeed, their views provide in themselves good evidence for the truth of Christian teaching: for, if their

---

4   Richard Dawkins in a lecture given at the Edinburgh International Science Festival, 1992. The reference is given in Alister McGrath, *Dawkins' God: Genes, Memes, and the Meaning of Life* (Oxford: Blackwell Publishing, 2005), p. 84 (note 6, 171).

5   Richard Dawkins again.

views about Christianity can be shown to be profoundly mistaken, they are exactly what a Christian would predict that many 'smart' people would want to believe.

Another claim that is made is that a secular view of life is morally superior to the Christian one. I will argue the exact opposite: that secular convictions are not particularly rational, if followed consistently, that they often lead to destructive practices, and that they cannot be followed coherently in everyday practice. I will offer illustrations of these claims.

What is truth?

It is not difficult to show that the notion of truth is one of the most important features of life. For example, all serious religious believers and atheists are convinced that the tenets they live by are true. However sceptical people may be about certain beliefs, it is impossible for human beings to reason or make choices without assuming that truth exists and can be known. In order to doubt or contradict other people's views, one must hold to one's own with a greater assurance of their validity.

Truth refers to a belief or statement about an event or fact that *corresponds to* or *matches* the reality to which it refers. For example, the statement, 'it is the case that this morning at exactly 9.34 am it started to rain' is true only if the first drops of rain reached the ground when the atomic clock registered that exact time. Truth is verified by checking out the accuracy of a certain set of circumstances: for example, in the report, 'my aunt has just been diagnosed with pancreatic cancer' can be demonstrated to be true by reference to a scan or x-ray showing a growth in the pancreatic region, later confirmed by a biopsy to be malignant.

This understanding of the meaning of truth (often called the 'correspondence' theory) is applied rigorously in a court of law. Statements, purporting to be true, made by witnesses and counsels for the prosecution and defence, have to be supported by incontrovertible evidence (beyond all reasonable doubt) in order to be accepted as actually being the case. For example, someone accused of murder may be able to provide a cast-iron alibi that he was fifty miles from the scene of the killing at the time it happened. His statement that he could not have committed the crime can be shown to be true by both independent, trustworthy witnesses and other circumstances that prove he was engaged in another activity in another location at that precise moment.

Some intellectual dilettantes argue that there is no such thing as truth. There is, they say, only our version of events or our opinions, which we project onto incidents or circumstances through our subjective experience. However, only foolish people would deny the objectivity of truth, and the possibility of its discovery, when trying to prove their innocence in the face of being falsely accused of a crime. As a theory of the meaning of truth, the correspondence theory is the only one available. Other theories may tackle the problem of adjudicating the evidence for truth claims. However, strictly speaking, they are not descriptions. This is a supremely important fact, when dealing with probable cases of the miscarriage of justice.

Non-empirical statements and truth

The situation of the nature of truth becomes more complicated when we move from statements about events in the world to statements about aesthetic judgements, moral values and religious beliefs. The following are some examples:

- The 'Hallelujah Chorus' (or anyone's favourite piece of music) is the most stirring piece of music ever composed

- Sexual relations outside of marriage are wrong

- To pay men and women different salaries for doing the same job is unjust

- Christ died to atone for our sins

- The cause of suffering is a craving for sense pleasure (the 'second noble truth' of Buddhism)

These kinds of statements could be multiplied. Their truth claims may well be fervently adhered to or, alternatively, disputed. To demonstrate which, if any, are true to reality is complicated, just because there is no overwhelming evidence that compels their acceptance.

Truth in the context of moral judgements

How human beings act as individuals and as societies, and why, is of the utmost importance. However, the question as to whether there are wholly objective, indisputably right or wrong ways of conducting life (independently of time and place) is hard to resolve.

Nevertheless, there is a growing consensus (evidenced by grass-roots campaigning groups) that certain ways of acting define what it means to behave in a civilised manner. For example, ordinary people, by an overwhelming majority, would condemn as morally unacceptable political and economic corruption, abusive physical and mental violence against vulnerable people (such as the mistreatment of the elderly or sexual harm against children), the exploitation of labour through excessively low wages and long hours, bonded labour, the avoidance of paying taxes, and many more activities, such as those that deny a fundamental right to be free from excessive state, media or electronic intrusion into private lives.

Attention to human rights, enshrined in Universal Declarations, Charters and Codes of Practice implies common norms shared across societies and cultures. The language of 'the common good' and 'human flourishing' presupposes that human beings, by virtue of their humanity, possess inherent dignity and worth which demand respect. At the same time, it has to be admitted that there is not always complete agreement on the extent of universal rights. In a good number of nations, women are not treated as fully equal with men (for example, in matters of education, marriage and inheritance). In Western nations, the unborn child can legally be deprived of the basic right to life,[6] if the woman carrying the foetus decides to exercise her lawfully permitted choice to end her pregnancy. The choice to terminate life has now, arbitrarily and against internationally binding Conventions, been accorded the status of a right.[7]

Truth in the context of religious beliefs

Even a superficial study of the core beliefs of the major world religions shows that there are many fundamental contradictions between them. One example, to illustrate this, is the divergent understandings of the role

---

[6] Against Article 3 of *The Universal Declaration of Human Rights.* The Preamble to the United Nations *Convention on the Rights of the Child* states that "child includes the child before as well as after the birth".

[7] I will consider the subject of rights further in Chapter 5.

of the prophet in Christianity and Islam. In the Bible, a clear line is drawn between the ruler and the prophet (for example, between David, the king, and Nathan, the prophet); the prophet acts as God's spokesperson to hold the ruling authority to account.[8] In Islam, by contrast, the supreme prophet (Muhammed), on moving from Mecca to Medina (the *hijrah*), became both ruler of the city, chief commander of the army and remained a prophet. There was no separate office to counterbalance the exercise of power.

If one accepts the logic of the law of non-contradiction – in other words, that all statements are either true or false (they cannot be true and false at the same time), either the view of Christianity or that of Islam about the prophetic office is true, or both are wrong. Atheists, espousing a secular religion, obviously believe the latter is true.

The issue of truth and error will not go away. It has a very public face. If something is true, it is true for the whole of life, public and private. Neither religious nor secular belief can be privatised, nor can they be treated as equally true or equally false; to do so, would beg the question about the nature of truth. In modern societies, particularly in the realm of moral values, issues of truth are both fundamental and controversial. Can the dilemma be solved?

Dialogue in the context of truth

In the experimental sciences, one of the main methods of assessing the outcomes of research work is called 'Inference to the Best Explanation' (IBE) – technically called *abduction*. It is a mode of reasoning that infers the truth of a situation on the grounds that a particular hypothesis offers the best explanation of the greatest amount of evidence relevant to the case. Thus, for example, in the medical sciences, a particular diagnosis of an illness is adopted because it offers the best explanation (cause) of the symptoms manifested.

IBE is a tool, used by reason, for settling the truth of a matter. It is essentially evidence-based: beginning with the evidence available to us,

---

[8]   Apart from Nathan's rebuke of David for committing adultery with Bathsheba and having her husband, Uriah, killed (2 Sam 12: 1–10), there is the equally famous case of Elijah denouncing the king, Ahab, and Jezebel, his wife, for the murder of Naboth and the theft of his property (1 Kings 21: 1–26).

we infer what would, if true, provide the *best* explanation of that evidence; taking into account all relevant information; *best* implies the most persuasive among possible alternative explanations.

It is legitimate to claim that IBE is the most adequate way of engaging in dialogue between the Christian faith and the claims of other religions or secular beliefs. It proceeds in a way similar to the proceedings of the law courts, with the aim of establishing 'beyond all reasonable doubt' (or at least, 'on the balance of probability') the truth of the matter (the motive, the opportunity, the nature of the crime itself, the likely perpetrator), relating to a particular belief, moral conviction or, in the case of the legal system, a crime.

Dialogue as a tool of Christian advocacy

Luke, the author of the book called *The Acts of the Apostles*, frequently uses the word *dialogemai* (to 'dialogue') as a method employed by Paul in his teaching and preaching ministry. It is translated into English in a variety of versions of the Bible by words such as, 'conduct a discussion', 'agree a case', 'debate', 'convince'. Paul 'dialogued' in synagogues, on the Areopagus in Athens (debating with Stoic and Epicurean philosophers), in the public lecture hall of Tyrannus in Ephesus, and in the trial before the Roman governor Festus and King Agrippa.[9] In this final example, Paul declares to Festus, 'I am speaking the sober truth' and to King Agrippa, in response to the question, 'are you so quickly persuading me to become a Christian?' 'I pray to God that not only you but also all who are listening to me today might become such as I am' (Acts 26:25, 28–29).

IBE as a method of advocacy

'Inference to the Best Explanation' is a tool that can help to demonstrate that the Christian faith is the best of all possible explanations for the way humans uniquely experience the universe, because it offers the most consistent, coherent and complete account. The theory's explanatory power is measured by its success in accounting for the data of experience, observation, historical witness and conduct. It is also successful in its

---

[9] See, Acts 17:2, 17; 18:4, 19; 19:8–10; 20:7, 9; 24:12, 25; 26:24–29.

predictive ability with regard to human behaviour: for example, in being able to explain why children who are deprived of proper care, security and affection by both a male and female parent are likely to suffer destructive consequences for their emotional stability or why watching pornographic material on the internet or gambling to excess causes mental distress. Its advantages are:

- It is based on evidence that is open to being rationally assessed and empirically tested

- It is open for anyone to participate in its conversational method

- It is applicable to many disciplines, thus it commands wide acceptance as a method of checking truth claims

- It avoids begging questions about whether basic beliefs have to be agreed prior to any dialogue taking place – although they may be disputed, they can still be brought into any discussion as potential explanations of human life

- It starts from the assumption that everyone is a part of the same nature of reality, about which discussions of truth can then be openly discussed

- It avoids an immediate appeal to subjective experience which, because it is hard to assess and may not be easy to communicate, makes genuine dialogue problematical[10]

So, IBE offers an excellent, tried and tested method for rationally considering all claims to know the ultimate reality that lies behind being human. Its process is one of advocacy in which alternative explanations of the great questions of existence are promoted, discussed, evaluated, and accepted or rejected. This will be the method that I will seek to adopt in the discussions that make up the content of this book.

Questions for reflection

1. Why is advocacy (apologetics) an important part of Christian witness?

---

[10] As is the case with a claim made by any person who asserts that they have been born in the wrong body as far as gender is concerned. Such a claim does not measure up to the truth of the case, for this can only be decided by their physiological reality.

2. Why do you think that some people (including some Christians) believe that the use of reason is harmful to faith or that faith inhibits the right use of reason?

3. It is quite common today to hear or read the phrase, 'there is no such thing as truth'. Why do you think people make this claim?

4. In a world full of diverse beliefs and political persuasions, how would you try to persuade someone that some attitudes and practices are morally right and some wrong?

5. It was claimed by a nineteenth-century philosopher that it is always and everywhere wrong to believe any statement on the basis of insufficient evidence. What kind of evidence would persuade you that the claims of Christianity are adequate and, therefore, more likely to be true than false?

2. Origins and Identity: the Fount of Reality and Recognition of the Self

This chapter is about origins and identity. Its purpose is offer credible answers to the questions: Why are we here? and Who are we? In accordance with the method of reasoning adopted for the book as a whole, it will review contrasting explanations for the existence of the universe, the emergence of life and of human beings as a unique and qualitatively different species from all others. It will, therefore, consider belief in the creation of the universe and all life by a personal divine being and the alternatives proposed by those who do not believe there is a God. It will draw out the implications of both views for the human search for identity.

In the beginning

For our purposes, we will consider two main accounts: the biblical and the scientific. This chapter will attempt to unravel some difficult and controversial issues which some people believe compel a choice between the creation narratives in Genesis 1–2 and modern scientific theories. Sadly, due to much misunderstanding on both sides of the debate, they are often portrayed as alternatives, meaning that they cannot both be true. Rightly understood, however, there is no conflict between the two. They are complementary, not incompatible, descriptions. Contrary views often arise because people hold contradictory presuppositions, which they are not willing readily to relinquish.

Origins: the biblical creation narrative

What do the stories of the first two chapters of the Bible tell us about our existence? They are certainly rich in teaching about the meaning of life. I will suggest nine affirmations.

- The existence of the universe is the result of a deliberate act of creation. Nothing is here by pure chance, but by the will and imagination of a supreme Being, who exists eternally, prior to all material reality.

- This Being is personal. He created by speaking: the phrase 'and God

17

said ... and it was so' occurs frequently in the opening chapter of the Bible (for example, Genesis 1:6–7). Speaking is a social activity, which assumes interpersonal communication. It is, therefore, not surprising to find the narrative affirming a plurality of persons within the reality of God, when it records God speaking in the first-person plural, 'let *us* make humankind in *our* image' (Genesis 1:26).

- Human existence is meaningful, special and precious. Humans have been given specific tasks to fulfil: to have dominion over the earth, by using the natural world to fulfil their needs; to be fruitful and multiply, by marrying and creating families, and to create a weekly rhythm of work and rest.

- Human beings, without exception, should be treated with equal dignity and honour. All have been given a special status or endowment by their creator, which demands respect.

- Human beings are given the responsibility of caring for the planet, not exploiting it out of greed. The habitat into which they are born, grow up and exercise their vocation is a gift from a good and generous creator. Human beings, therefore, are given the role of being trustees, handing on a well-tended world to the next generation.

- The universe exhibits imagination and design. In its origin it was created perfect. Therefore, the imperfections that are all too obvious today need to be explained.

- Men and women are born equal in their vocations, in dignity, worth and sacredness. In Genesis 2, the woman is created as a 'help-meet' or 'companion' for the man. He is ish (the male); she is isha (the female). The two sexes are intended to complement one another; neither is superior to the other. They form the most basic community, which functions productively only in the context of a completely harmonious relationship of mutual esteem and reciprocal responsibilities. Full sexual intimacy is intended to be consummated only within a formalised (marriage) relationship between a man and a woman, intended to last for the duration together of the lives of both spouses.

- Human flourishing is dependent on maintaining the right balance between work and rest. According to the creation narrative, together with the blessing pronounced over all aquatic creatures and birds (the first animate creatures commanded to be fruitful and multiply), the human couple and the seventh day also receive a blessing (Gen. 1: 21-22; 1:28; 2:3).

- The whole human race has a common ancestry. This implies that all races, ethnic groups, peoples and nations are of the same stock. There may be a variety of skin colours, human characteristics and cultural expressions distributed throughout humankind, but these do not infer some kind of intrinsic intellectual, moral or spiritual ranking.

This account of origins is wholly unique. It is not matched in any other religious tradition. It has had an immense impact on how humans view themselves and conduct their lives. If the first two chapters of Genesis were to be removed from the Bible, as if they never existed, or if their teaching were to be rejected as a legendary saga, without any substance, we would live in a very different world. It is, unfortunately, the kind of world in which many young people grow up, ignorant of the truth of who they really are. It is not surprising, therefore, that many struggle with a crisis of identity. They lack any substantial and accurate framework for understanding what it means to be human.

Origins: modern scientific narratives

With regard to present scientific knowledge, there is no controversy about the fact that the universe had a beginning in one singular act, known colloquially as 'the Big Bang'. It is true that not all scientists are wholly comfortable with the idea. However, their discomfort has little to do with the possession of a plausible, alternative, scientific version of the inauguration of the universe, but with the implication that something or someone, beyond all material existence, must have caused it. For people predisposed to dismiss the existence of a supreme, eternally-subsisting Being, this is bound to be troubling. Denial of a creator-god (atheism), however, has nothing to do with knowledge that is ascertainable through strictly scientific methods of investigation. Most scientists agree that the evidence for one sole act of birth (of the universe) amounts to proof. Alternative theories, such as a steady-state universe or multi-universes are largely discounted, because they are purely speculative.

Alternative theories concerning 'the history of time'[11]

As has been pointed out, there are only two possible assumptions concerning existence. The first is the *naturalist* belief – that there is nothing whatsoever beyond or behind the universe, that matter is all that there is, and that, therefore, everything can be explained by exploring natural laws.[12] The second theory is the *supranaturalist* conviction that ultimate reality is non-material – the universe came into existence at a singular point of time, caused by a non-material power and, therefore, there is a beyond and a behind.

Given that there was a beginning to all physical existence (before the 'Big Bang' absolutely nothing material existed), what is the most reasonable explanation of this event? Stephen Hawking says, 'In real time, the universe has a beginning and an end at singularities (i.e., a point) that form a boundary to space–time and at which laws of science break down.'[13]

It is a fact, then, that before this singular point, absolutely nothing physical existed. Then, suddenly, something occurred that caused a chain reaction that brought the expanding universe into existence. But it is evident that something cannot come out of nothing. Whatever begins to exist has to have a cause. If the universe had a beginning, there was a cause. This is an inescapable conclusion of everything we know about reality.

Scientists are the last people who would deny the logic of the argument, for science would be impossible if objects could suddenly spring into existence without any possible prior agency. It follows that those whose creed is naturalism either have to remain agnostic about a first cause, or invent some other explanation – for example, physical laws, gravity, a

---

[11]   This phrase is taken from Stephen Hawking's best-selling book *A Brief History of Time.*
[12]   I am using the term 'naturalist' in a narrower sense than 'secularist.' It refers to the belief that everything is reducible ultimately to the workings of a natural order, explicable entirely within a structure of laws formulated within an assumption that all of reality is enclosed in one gigantic material existence. In this sense, 'materialist' is an equivalent term.
[13]   Stephen Hawking, *A Brief History of Time: From the Big Bang to Black Holes* (London: Bantam Books, 1988), p. 139.

fluctuation in a quantum vacuum or another. However, any alternative explanation only pushes the question of the origin of all things one step further back.

John Lennox (Professor of Mathematics in the University of Oxford) explains the irony of the situation produced by this controversy. In the sixteenth century, some Christian leaders tried to resist advances in science (Galileo and all that), because scientists seemed to threaten Christian belief (as formulated at that time). Today, however, predominant scientific ideas about the beginning of all things are resisted because they threaten atheism and increase the plausibility of belief in God!

As far as present knowledge is concerned, denial of an act of creation by a spiritual being has nothing to do with scientifically demonstrated evidence; it has everything to do with a prior belief that the notion of a creative act cannot be accepted, because of the consequences it entails. To the unbiased mind that wishes to judge the arguments soberly and without prior prejudices, everything seems to confirm the opening words of the Bible, 'In the beginning God created...'

Even atheists seem to admit that there had to be an original cause, outside of time and space, of the inception of all things, though not necessarily with attributes usually ascribed to the God of the Bible. If not the God of the Bible, then who or what? As there is no reason, deducible from scientific methods of investigation, to preclude such a God, what other reasons could there be? It is reasonable to conclude that the atheists' (and, to a slightly lesser extent, the agnostics') thinking about the origin of the universe springs from the desire to maintain a notion of human freedom as unconstrained self-determination. The existence of a God who, assuming he is the morally perfect giver and upholder of life, is able to make demands, threatens humans' autonomy, free from being accountable to anyone except themselves.

Alternative theories concerning the history of planet earth

When we explore possible explanations for the origin of life on earth and the emergence of homo sapiens, three possible views are promoted as the most credible.

Atheistic evolution

Everything that exists or has existed is the result of an evolutionary process with three parts:

- random variation or mutation

- natural selection

- common descent

Often evolution is described as the 'survival of the fittest' through adaptation. It is said that within nature there exists a mechanism that guarantees that only organisms that adapt successfully to the changing circumstances of their environment continue to replicate. This theory states that the whole process is blind – there is no design, no purpose, it has all happened by chance. A god-hypothesis to explain the formation and growth of animate creatures is unnecessary. If there were to be a 'watchmaker', needed to explain what might at first sight appear to be evidence of design, it would be blind. Everything can be explained by an impersonal evolutionary process that has left behind plenty of clues as to how it has happened.

Theistic evolution

Many Christian scientists, theologians and others believe that the mechanism of natural selection is a correct way of describing the development of life-forms. They accept the notion of common ancestry, often portrayed in the image of a 'tree of life' (with one set of roots and trunk, but many branches): all living matter comes from one single source and, over billions of years, has evolved and diversified through constant small changes. At the same time, the Christian who accepts evolution believes that God has been involved in the process at every step of the way. God created the evolutionary mechanism; it has been his method for producing change and variation. Design is not an illusion. God's existence and his purposes can be deduced from observation of the natural world.[14]

---

[14] In a highly sophisticated and abstract argument, William A. Dembski, maintains that both natural evidence and rational thought point unmistakeably to the priority of information over matter as the basic reality

Intelligent design

Other theists are sceptical about the standard evolutionary story, particularly the theory of common descent (often referred to as macro-evolution). They allege that there are several insurmountable difficulties in accepting a neo-Darwinian evolutionary theory:

- *The origin of life:* For life to have arisen from inanimate matter, there would have needed to have been a prior input in the form of coded information which issued instructions. This suggests an intelligence of some kind operating.

- *The origin of the human species:* On the basis of an impersonal beginning to existence plus time plus chance, the gradual evolution of myriads of species to form one particular species so qualitatively different from every other seems wholly implausible. Human beings possess consciousness, a mind, the ability to reason abstractly, a sense of self-hood, an ability to plan for the future, the experience of free will, the intuition of the existence of an objective moral order and an appreciation of beauty. Human beings represent a qualitative leap in the so-called 'chain of existence', which no amount of time on its own could have produced through an impersonal, fortuitous operation. Such a distinctive kind of entity as a human being with the characteristics outlined above requires a theory of intervention to make sense of experience.

- *The inability of science to produce convincing evidence of macro-evolution:* There does not appear to be any cogent evidence within the fossil record that speciation has taken place. No evidence of the development of one species into another (in other words, intermediate forms) has been discovered hitherto. This lack of testimony seems staggeringly unlikely if evolution occurred at a macro-level. Natural selection does not produce new species. It is

---

of the universe. Information presupposes intelligence and a purpose-driven process of the development of diversity. Intelligence indicates the probability of what we would describe as an entity capable of rational decision-making. By analogy from human experience, it is not a huge step to posit the likelihood of there being a personal intelligent being involved in the origin and continuation of the universe. See William Dembski, *Being as Communion: A Metaphysics of Information* (Farnham: Ashgate Publishing, 2014).

worth noting that mutations may be regressive as well as advantageous: in other words, a constant, inevitable, upward development of forms from the lower to the higher is not born out by the facts.

- *Complexity.* It is inconceivable, however much time one may allow, for random mutations in a totally chance process to have produced an organ as intricate as the human brain with its incredibly creative possibilities. Even with an immense amount of time and an incalculable number of participants, monkeys could never produce a play like Shakespeare's *Hamlet* by typing individual letters haphazardly.

Thus, all that can be accepted so far, on the basis of reliable evidence, is micro-evolution – in other words, the development of characteristics *within* species. Such a theory can be shown to be probable through the evidence provided by successful selective breeding. The question of how exactly billions of living species have come into existence can be left, for the moment, as an open question.

So who are we?

Human beings tend to find their identity initially in their immediate origin. In what circumstances did they come into the world? Who are their biological father and mother? Why did they come together to produce me? Where was I born? What is my racial, ethnic and national background? Many people are interested to know the details of their ancestry, as attested to by the popular TV programme, *Who Do You Think You Are?*

What about the beginning of all origins? As we have been discussing, there appear to be only two alternatives: either the universe, including our amazing planet, was conceived, planned and created by some power existing prior to its existence; or, somehow, it generated itself. In the latter case, the way it happened has to remain a mystery, seeing that there does not appear to be any possible, adequate cause.

So, our present existence, especially life itself and the astonishing reality of human beings, has to be explained on one or other assumption: 'in the beginning God...', or 'in the beginning nothing...' We have already reviewed the consequences of accepting the evidence that points to the reality of an eternally self-existing, personal creator fully able to carry out his will, in accordance with his character. If, on the other hand, the creator's existence is rejected, seen only as a projection of human beings apparent inherent need to believe in something greater than themselves, the consequences that flow are entirely different.

The consequences of atheism: three enigmas

- There can be no explanation of why the universe exists, rather than nothing existing.

- There is no explanation of how living organisms have been derived from inanimate matter, seeing that life had to precede the transition from one to the other. Nobody has come close to solving the question of how self-generating, self-organising living things arose spontaneously out of non-living substances, seeing that information encoded in DNA is needed for life to be generated. The most plausible explanation, once the dogma of materialism is challenged, is that this information had to be introduced from outside the process.

- Life has no intrinsic meaning. The stark, bleak and depressing statement echoes down the ages:

  In a universe of blind physical forces and genetic replication ... you won't find any rhyme or reason in it, nor any justice. The universe we observe had precisely the properties we should expect if there is, at bottom, no design, no purpose, no evil and no good, nothing but blind pitiless indifference.[15]

In spite of this highly dismal view of existence, the naturalist account of evolution talks about the whole process being geared to the survival of certain species, those able to adapt themselves most successfully to the circumstances of their environment. Does not survival suggest an objective, a goal towards which living beings are programmed to respond? In the way that it is presented in most mainstream accounts of evolution

---

[15] Richard Dawkins, *River Out of Eden* (New York: Basic Books, 1995), p. 133.

it appears to be the case that survival is the great engine that drives development in a progressively upward direction.

However, in this account, survival is invested with more weight than it can bear; it is merely a description of what has come to pass. It is a truism of observation. The fact that we can talk about survival is due to the fact that we have survived! Unlike all other living species, humans can reflect on why they alone can talk about survival. Is this really the only possible reason for existing, that living beings may go on existing? Then, creating our own reasons to exist sounds like making the best of a bad job. There is no intrinsic value in either what we are or do, for we are not fulfilling any specified destiny. On the contrary, according to this thesis we are, of all creatures, the most miserable.

If the *only value* produced by a blind, chance process is survival, and only the fittest survive, why not practise eugenics? This could happen deliberately through the mandatory abortion of all babies with defects that might weaken resistance to certain diseases, and therefore contribute to a diminishing chance of survival, and moreover, use up valuable medical resources in the attempt to keep the infant alive. Or, it could come about through a programme of selective breeding, and the culling of babies that did not measure up to stringent standards of what constitutes a strong, healthy, constitution.

I would strongly argue that a naturalistic account of evolution has no basis for affirming the intrinsic worth of human beings – that is that they possess a value that does not depend on their attributes but inheres in them as humans, beings essentially different from even the highest primates. Let us take the example of how we treat animals and the way we deal with human beings. We talk about having pet animals (dogs, cats, horses, etc.) being 'put down' when their lives are no longer sustainable. Yet, most people still view the calculated ending of human life (euthanasia) through the injection by a medical professional of a lethal drug as abhorrent, just because medical practice is based on protecting and preserving, not terminating, human life. Well may Charles Darwin have given his second major book the title of *The Descent of Man*! Dostoevsky, the brilliant Russian author, observed, 'if God does not exist, everything is permitted.'

Questions for reflection

1. Why do some people believe there is a conflict between the Bible and science over the origin of the world?

2. What does the biblical account of creation tell us that we could not learn elsewhere?

3. Why do you think some people are so opposed to belief in creation by God?

4. What do you make of the belief that all life on earth evolved from single cells, without any further acts of creation?

5. How would you persuade someone that the world is the result of God's will and design?

3. Good and Evil: the Field of Human Conflict

Moral relativism

It is common today for many people to claim that there are no absolute, universal standards of right and wrong by which good and evil can be judged. Those who make this claim are moral relativists. They hold that the morality of all acts depends entirely on the circumstances in which they are performed. Categorical, unquestionable and definitive demands made on us to behave in certain ways simply do not exist. Such a view means that it is impossible to make absolute distinctions, valid in all situations, between what is virtuous and what immoral.

Although this attitude is widespread in contemporary secular societies, in practice, no-one is a consistent relativist. Everyone, at some point, will act according to some unconditional, moral norm. The fact that some norms seem to the majority of people to be utterly depraved – for example, the desire of some extreme Muslims to forbid the education of girls, or the policy of some governments to suppress the use of minority languages – shows that those who condemn these decrees are not relativists.

Relativism is, of course, self-contradictory: anyone who holds the view that there are no absolute ethical norms is making a claim that, presumably, they believe to be universally valid. So, when anyone says that their moral beliefs are right for them personally, but not necessarily for others, and then go on to criticise actions they take to be morally repugnant, they display considerable confusion. Moral relativism may sound beautifully tolerant – but in the real world, everyone will make exceptions to their tolerance. To advocate non-judgemental attitudes towards others appears to be worthy of praise. However, as it is virtually impossible not to evaluate the ethical standards that drive other people's motives and actions, the sentiment becomes largely theoretical.

The reality of goodness and wickedness

Atheists and agnostics often point out that they are likely to be just as morally upright as people who believe in God. They affirm that to behave

28

with honesty, compassion, kindness and consideration for the needs of others does not require belief in a supreme ruler of the universe, who has laid down a set of moral laws to be obeyed. Indeed, they would go on to argue that obedience to commands and rules, out of fear of punishment, is not a particularly high moral way of acting.

People will be known by the virtuous or vicious fruits produced in their lives. Most people, unless suffering from a severe personality disorder, recognise goodness and wickedness. At the level of describing what happens in many cases this is a correct observation. However, there are a considerable number of disputed moral issues, where clever people come to profoundly different conclusions: the life and death cases of abortion and euthanasia spring to mind.

When speaking about evil, many refer straightaway to the various genocides that have taken place in the twentieth century – for example the massacre of Armenians in Turkey during and just after the first World War (1915–19), the 'final solution' of the Nazi regime, the Pol Pot 'killing fields' of Cambodia, Rwanda in the mid-1990s, Srebrenica in Bosnia, and others. Each one of these witnessed a determined attempt to eliminate a whole human community on the basis of its specific characteristics. The slaughter was accompanied by unbridled cruelty and callousness, when those in power subjected certain ethnic, politically motivated or religious groups to unimaginable suffering for the sheer pleasure of causing them pain and humiliating them. The evil shown consists not just in causing distress and torment, but in the delight experienced in causing it.

In the case of goodness, it is common to identify supremely sacrificial acts made on behalf of others: for example, in exposing oneself to danger by rescuing someone from drowning or being attacked; searching for survivors after an earthquake; offering the transplant of a kidney or bone marrow for another's well-being; care given to elderly neighbours or disabled children. The examples could be multiplied. We recognise instantly that such acts of kindness and generosity are wholly unselfish.

For the rest of this chapter, I want to concentrate more on the reality of evil because, for most non-Christians, it is much more problematical than goodness, and we need to try to understand why. Many people believe that humans are born into the world essentially good. If this is one's belief, then accounting for the existence of evil constitutes a quandary. There does not seem to be an adequate reason; evil just happens to be. We can recognise its existence but search fruitlessly for a convincing explanation.

The origin of evil

So, non-believers in God have a good idea of what is good and evil. But in the absence of a morally perfect divine creator, can they justify their beliefs? Their worldview is constructed on the basis that humans are the result of an evolutionary process without meaning; by an amazing set of circumstances and coincidences life, as we know it, exists by self-generation. The only built-in motivating power is survival, through the impulse to reproduce. If this is one's fundamental conviction, where does the notion of evil come from? Given the theory, it might be logical to conclude that the only evil we can talk about meaningfully is whatever hinders reproduction by the fittest.

As far as we know, animals have no sense of right and wrong, for they do not possess a moral faculty or conscience. Thus, if a dog kills a small child, we do not have it put down as an act of punishment, because it has knowingly transgressed the law, 'you shall not kill', but in order to stop another tragedy happening. Dogs are not responsible for their actions; we do not put them on trial. Rather, we hold their owners to account. However, on the naturalistic evolutionary hypothesis, human beings are merely animals that walk upright, have more complex brains and more dexterity in their hands than all other mammals. How, we might ask, do these distinguishing marks give them a capacity for making moral judgements? In spite of these difficulties, attempts have been made to suggest possible causes of evil without reference to a God-shaped universe.

Naturalistic accounts of evil

We will examine three different attempts to provide a plausible explanation of evil from a non-theistic perspective.

Ervin Staub, in his book, *The Roots of Evil: The Origins of Genocide and Other Group Violence*, locates evil, in the first instance, in acts of hate-speech, characterised by stereotyping, scapegoating and demonising others as enemies, leading to exploitation, the suppression of rights and even elimination.[1] Such acts are often symptomatic, he says, of authoritarian regimes with a culture of the 'strong leader'. They are characterised by their pursuit of extremely aggressive policies towards weaker groups, whom they see as threats to their power and privileges as the ruling elite.

These, and other instances of evil arise, he says, out of difficult life conditions experienced by those who perpetrate them: for example, violence suffered in childhood, growing up in a dysfunctional family with a tragic absence of genuine affection, fear of a loss of privileges and livelihood, the breakdown of trust, a loss of self-respect and, ultimately, the collapse of a law-abiding, civil society. He speaks of a continuum of destruction marked by cumulative choices, decisions and acts:

> A society that has long devalued a group and discriminated against its members, has strong respect for authority, and has an overly superior and/or vulnerable self-concept, is more likely to turn against a sub-group.[2]

In response to his theories, we should point out that they are the result of two confusions. Firstly, he has muddled up *circumstances* that favour the spread of evil (for example, prolonged campaigns of hate against groups collectively held responsible for some ill-defined offence) with the *causes* of evil. Secondly, he has analysed the *mechanisms* that perpetrate evil (that is, how evil is manifest in the world) with the *origin* of evil. What he has not explained are the reasons why people would be driven to choosing the evil of aggression and violence in addressing their own experience of gratuitous suffering, rather than goodwill, understanding, peace and kindness. In other words, he needs an adequate explanation of the instinct to repay evil with evil – to retaliate through exercising revenge.

Simon Baron-Cohen, in his book, *Science of Evil: On Empathy and the Origins of Cruelty,* believes that the basic cause of evil is the loss in the individual and community of *affective empathy*.[3] This can be understood as the capacity to appreciate the feelings of others and identify

---

[1]   Ervin Staub, *The Roots of Evil: The Origins of Genocide and Other Group Violence* (Cambridge: Cambridge University Press, 1989).

[2]   Staub, *Roots of Evil,* p. 5.

[3]   Simon Baron-Cohen, *Science of Evil: On Empathy and the Origins of Cruelty* (New York: Basic Books, 2011).

sympathetically and supportively with their situation. Empathy requires the ability to step outside ourselves and our needs and sensitively into the world of another person or group.

He maintains that the basis of empathy can be discovered in the workings of the brain. The erosion of empathy can be caused by biological determinants, such as certain medical conditions, or social factors, such as trauma and stress.

There is some truth in what he says as a description of what occurs when evil is perpetrated: empathy is absent, because it has been trampled upon. Therefore, it becomes much easier to treat others as much less than fully human. However, to describe cruelty, arising out of a loss of empathy, as the supreme example of evil does not offer an explanation of evil as such. On this account, evil is just a reality of life; a way, perhaps, of trying to cope with exceptionally harsh adverse circumstances that some human beings have been through. Its origin, however, is incomprehensible, just because cruelty does not have to be a response to the hurt one has suffered at the hands of others.

Moreover, to trace the operation and location of brain signals in the cortex of the brain, when empathy is present or absent is not to be confused with providing a cause. Electrical impulses in the brain may accompany human moods and emotions; they do not cause them directly in most cases.

Paul Bloom in his study, *Just Babies: The Origins of Good and Evil*, acknowledges that a naturalist has to attempt to explain how a moral sense might have arisen and developed either in evolutionary biology or social psychology.[4] No other option is an open possibility. Neuroscientists, he affirms, can look at parts of the brain involved in moral reasoning; sociologists may explore how features of the environment encourage kindness or cruelty.

His own research into how very young children, even those of less than one year, react to examples of moral goodness and badness incline him to believe that moral discernment is innate from the beginning of a child's existence. Humans are simply endowed with a capacity to distinguish

---

4   Paul Bloom, *Just Babies: The Origins of Good and Evil* (London: The Bodley Head, 2013).

between kind and cruel actions, have compassion, and a sense of fairness and justice. However, this innate goodness is limited by self-interest, indifference to the needs and plight of others, hostility to strangers, bigotry and disgust. He quotes a statement of Thomas Jefferson:

> Man was destined for society. His morality, therefore, was to be formed to this object. He was endowed with a sense of right and wrong relative to this. This sense is as much part of his nature, as the sense of hearing, seeing, feeling; it is the true foundation of morality.[5]

He seems to be talking about conscience. However, this does not solve the conundrum, for how can a moral foundation be a product of evolution? How is it possible for the wholly amoral force of natural selection to produce a sense of moral convictions? This is the mystery that naturalists have not been able to solve convincingly. If moral intuition is innate from birth, it is the foundation on which moral education is built later; it does not arise out of the moral beliefs of particular societies. So, a convincing explanation of the origin of evil needs a 'horse' to be put before the 'cart'. These three theories merely attempt to explain the cart.

The Christian account of evil

Christians (and other theists) see evil in relation to an absolutely good God, who is the very definition of goodness. He created a world that 'was very good' (Genesis 1:31). So, it follows, if this is what really happened, that evil is an intrusion into an originally uncorrupted world; it was never an intrinsic part of the fabric of life. Only in the Bible do we find an account of evil that takes it back to the beginning of human existence. As the early Christian writer Paul puts it, 'sin entered the world through one man' (Romans 5:12).

So, the existence of evil presupposes a moral order, put in place by God to reflect his character. Just as the physical world functions according to physical laws that are not invented by humans, but are a given in nature, so humans function best when they adhere to God's moral laws, also part of the warp and woof of existence. Evil, then, is the result of human beings choosing to abandon God's directions for a full human life and deciding

---

5   Bloom, *Just Babies.*

to create their own kind of world. In a remarkable passage, Paul calls it an *exchange* (Romans 1: 22, 25, 26). People have exchanged the truth about God, creation and the path to right living for false beliefs they have invented. Evil, therefore, originated in the human race accepting a fundamental lie. People began to live on the basis of unreality.

According to the narrative which recounts the origin of evil (Genesis 2–3), evil entered the world as the abuse of freedom. We now call it human beings' desire to be autonomous.

The second account of creation in Genesis tells how God put the man and the woman whom he had formed into a lush garden. It contained all kinds of trees both ornamental ('pleasing to the eye') and edible ('good for food'). God gave one word of warning: 'you are free to eat of any tree in the garden, but you must not eat from the tree of the knowledge of good and evil, for when you eat of it you will surely die'. God has confirmed the principle that freedom is set within the ultimate bounds of a moral order. The special creatures he has put within the garden have immense freedom. They are 'free to eat of any tree in the garden'.

This is not imprisonment, restriction or petty-mindedness. The man and the woman may sample and experiment as far as they are able to wander. However, this freedom was not without limits. There was one boundary beyond which the pair might not trespass. Their well-being depended upon exercising their considerable freedom within this limitation. Erich Fromm is right, therefore, to point out that sinfulness arose directly from the original misuse of freedom.[6]

> By going beyond the limit, the first human pair broke the harmony of the created order and the result was a tragic disruption of the harmony of relationships'.[7]

The serpent's question, 'did God say...?' is the most fundamental temptation that humankind faces. The response can be, 'Yes, he did; it is for our maximum well-being'. Or, it could be, 'no he didn't.' Or, again, it might be, 'I don't care whether did or didn't, I will choose my own path through life.' Finally, and more likely in a secular environment, it is likely

---

6   Erich Fromm, *The Fear of Freedom*, (Abingdon, UK: Routledge Classics, 2001), p. 27.

7   J. Andrew Kirk, *The Meaning of Freedom: A Study of Secular, Muslim and Christian Views* (Carlisle: Paternoster Press, 1998), p. 202–203.

to be, 'as God does not exist, nor does any established moral order, we will have to invent a reply to the question as we go along.'

A blind, random, impersonal evolutionary process knows nothing of good and evil. In the eternal struggle for survival, morality has no place. At the same time, it occurs to humans that living in a 'condition of perpetual war of every person against every person'[8], 'a life [which is] solitary, poor, nasty, brutish, and short'[9] is not very satisfactory. So, they create an order of their own to limit and attempt to reverse their natural aggression.

It is interesting to note that Freud (the father of psychoanalysis)

> from the 1920s onwards ... in a somewhat dramatic change of direction added to the life-affirming stimuli of Eros the impulses towards death and destruction, which he referred to as Thanatos. The latter occupied his thought for the remaining years of his life and could be summed up in one word: aggression ... It is as powerful, if not more so, than Eros. It arises in part through the fact that all of human life is lived, consciously, within the inevitable horizon that death consummates existence. It manifests itself in guilt towards oneself, the result of the constant failures to live up to one's ego ideal, and in the destructive critique of others, whom one blames for one's own unhappiness.[10]

Todd Dufresne sums up Freud's ultimately tragic response to what he derived from his thinking about both psychoanalysis and the development of civilisation as he conceived them:

> Existence is ... the consequence of a battle between life and death drives ... the end of which is the termination of the seemingly interminable battle of drives.[11]

---

8 Thomas Hobbes, *Leviathan* (Harmondsworth, UK: Penguin Classics, 2016), part 1, Chapter 13.

9 Thomas Hobbes, *Leviathan* (Oxford: Oxford University Press, 1996), Chapter 13, p.62.

10 Kirk, *Being Human: An Historical Inquiry Into Who We Are* (Eugene, OR: Wipf and Stock, 2019) p. 273.

11 Todd Dufresne, *The Late Sigmund Freud: Or, the last Word on Psychoanalysis, Society and All the Riddles of Life* (Cambridge, CUP, 2017), p. 130.

Freud, one of the greatest thinkers of the twentieth century, bears witness from his own observations, to humans' innate drive towards aggression and the death instinct, resulting from the struggle to survive.

The problem of evil

We can conclude that evil presents a huge dilemma to non-believers in God: how to make any sense of it? It also causes great perplexity to Christians. If, as the Bible affirms, God created everything very good, and yet created it in such a way that evil and innocent suffering is possible, it would seem to lack perfection. If someone, not knowing anything of God, came from outer space to earth, he or she might conclude that whoever created the world made a mess of it. The experiment seems to have gone hopelessly wrong. Either God is not in control, or he is not morally virtuous. If he could have built a world without evil and suffering, but has not done so, does not evil, by default, originate in his will? This conundrum represents the Achilles' heel of the Christian claim to know the truth about God, life and death.

What response may be given to this great challenge? The following points summarise extremely briefly the main answers that have been given by Christians down the ages:

- Sin and evil are intrusions into the world as originally created. Christian faith uses the word 'fallen' to describe the fact that people do not think or behave as God intended. It follows that, if sin and evil are not natural, but historical failures, wrong can be righted. There is a proper ground for fighting against all forms of injustice, error and brutality. It makes sense, therefore, to call some beliefs and actions inhuman and inhumane. We can oppose evil, without running the risk of opposing God, since God hates evil far more intensely than we ever could.

- The assumption that a perfectly good God would prevent evil ever occurring is not necessarily correct. It is not self-evident that there could never be a sufficient reason for God to allow the possibility of evil to appear. It is perfectly reasonable to think that by eliminating evil altogether a greater good is lost, or even a greater evil is committed. One suggestion to account for the existence of evil is that, if it were wholly absent from thought and experience, the same would be true of goodness. The latter is characterised and morally accentuated by the reality of its opposite.

- In order for human beings to be free agents, not autonoma, the power of contrary choice is necessary; otherwise personal responsibility is a mirage. Free will is a reality of human behaviour. If it were not so, people could not be held to account. And if no-one is liable for their beliefs or actions, there could be no justice or injustice. Human society would descend into chaos. Free will is not a convenient illusion, concocted just in order that we may be able to control people's behaviour and legitimately punish wrongdoing and reward righteousness. To choose freely to be and do what we wish is attainable, even though there may be hindrances and constraints along the way. For these reasons, therefore, it is important that God has limited his power to overrule human choice.

- Were it not for the existence of evil, goodness would not be able to flourish. It is often said by ethicists that evil is the absence of the good. The reverse is also true: goodness is understood in contrast to wrongdoing; evil highlights its opposite. In the absence of evil, goodness is shorn of its sharpness and outstanding nature. We should not conclude, however, that evil is thereby justified, because it may promote a greater good.

- God has shown conclusively that he is not indifferent to the pain and suffering caused by evil. In Jesus Christ, God has freely exposed himself to and experienced the full horror of evil. He has born it in his own person and conquered it, and thus created a means of escaping its tragic consequences.

Questions for reflection

1. Why do you think moral relativism in our society is such a popular theory?
2. How would you define evil and goodness?
3. How would you evaluate the three attempts above by non-theists to explain the origin of evil?
4. How would you explain the biblical account of the origin of good and evil?
5. How does the problem of evil affect your faith in God?

4. Alienation and Reconciliation: Overcoming Evil and Promoting Goodness

Alienation as the cause of evil

We have established that the existence of good and evil in the world is real. There appears to be a huge contradiction in human nature: although, according to current research, humans recognise right and wrong from an early age, children still need teaching and discipline to set them on the right path and keep them there. We possess a conscience that stimulates sensitivity to right and wrong. Yet, if it is not maintained in good working order and continually fine-tuned, it loses its cutting edge. Especially when it comes to practising honesty and generosity towards others, it can be ignored or rejected; whereupon, it becomes increasingly less sensitive.

How we view the challenge of overcoming evil and promoting goodness depends on the diagnosis of the problem. Only by getting to the root cause is it possible to prescribe an appropriate cure. As we have seen, the Christian faith states that the basic problem lies in abusing our freedom by attempting to exchange God's world for one of our own creation. The principal result is alienation from the creator, from other human beings, from our own deepest moral aspirations (we experience pangs of guilt and shame) and from the environment.

Instead of seeing God as a friend and a helper, we view him as a rival. We experience a clash of wills, so we accuse God (quite unjustifiably) of limiting our freedom and stifling our enjoyment of life. We are estranged, having a completely false idea of the nature of God. We tend to picture him as an eternally vigilant policeman, whose main occupation is to monitor our every move (with a heavenly CCTV camera permanently turned on), so he can catch us unawares and punish us. Such an impression of God is completely false; it merely highlights our alienation.

The symptoms of alienation

We live in an abnormal situation. We experience broken relationships and long for healing and reconciliation; yet often we are not willing to pay the price. Alienation constitutes a powerful negative force in the way we

38

conduct our lives; yet, its hidden depths often go unrecognised.

- It is caused by our choices to live at a *distance* from others. As we do not live sufficiently close to them, we lack an appreciation of their lives. Hence, we are prone to listen to and believe the many misrepresentations, generalisations, prejudices, 'scapegoating' and even 'demonising' made of the other.

- So, we become *estranged* from them. We perceive them as threats. They are 'strange' people. They appear to us from the 'outside'. This can lead to a fear of what is foreign to us; it may even lead to a certain amount of paranoia about what they might do to us. In order to protect our interests and security, we may be led to exert force against those who we believe are likely to endanger our lives. Force does not necessarily mean physical violence or restraint. It could mean personal protection by inducing the state to change the law in favour of those who claim to be discriminated against.

- Alienation may lead to the *exploitation* of others, using them as instruments to fulfil our purposes. This is an abuse of power; it treats other people just as we would not want to be treated ourselves. This abuse may be legitimised by creating ideologies, doctrines, myths and even religions to justify what our consciences tell us is wrong.

- An abnormal situation is also characterised by *disorder* in society, demonstrated by a prevalence of communication breakdown, corruption and confusion. In such circumstances, false ideologies (for example, fascism, extreme nationalism, ethnic isolationism and religious supremacy) and destructive political movements may become attractive and proliferate. These ideologies and movements proclaim that they alone have the power to answer the breakdown of consensus, democratic values and respect for the rule of law in society. However, their ruthless extermination of all opposition leads to extreme polarisation and often leads to civil war (recently in the Balkans, Ukraine, Syria, Iraq, the Yemen and South Sudan).

Reconciliation – the remedy for alienation

The key to overcoming evil and promoting goodness is the restoration of right relationships. If it is true, as the Christian faith affirms, that the fundamental alienation is between us and God, the creator and sustainer of all things, then reconciliation needs to begin there. The good news is that God has taken the initiative and done everything necessary to rectify the situation. Starting with the history of Jesus, we can begin to understand what God has done on behalf of the whole of humanity.

Jesus Christ is the one and only human being who has ever walked on this earth who was a model of a normal and normative life, as it was intended to be. He knew in practice the deep causes of alienation – such as fear, feelings of insecurity and hatred. He experienced personally the anger and enmity of his opponents and the fear and disloyalty of his friends. In other words, he entered fully into an alienated world, full of conflicts, dishonesty, self-righteousness and hypocrisy. In this sense, there was nothing idealistic or romantic about his life. He encountered the real world in all its multiple examples of corruption.

Faced by the reality of Jesus' total goodness, which exposed their rotten lives and challenged their self-interests, the religious and political authorities of the time reacted with immense antagonism towards him; they had Jesus judicially murdered on false charges. His crucifixion (an instance of extreme cruelty, which happened to be the means the Roman empire used to carry out the death penalty) represented the supreme place and moment of the world's alienation. There, Jesus took on himself all the evil that human beings could throw at him.

The death of Jesus designated the supreme moment of absolute abnormality. In the cry of desolation from the cross, 'My God, my God, why have you forsaken me?' (Mark 15:34) humanity's total estrangement from the unconditional goodness of God was enacted. The curse of abnormality as born to the uttermost (Gal 3:13); it was taken into the heart of God, between the Father and the Son.

There had to be a momentary separation, for 'God made him (Jesus) to be sin who knew no sin' (2 Corinthinas 5:21), so that human beings might be freed from both the guilt and power of sin. This sacrificial act demonstrates how profoundly sin has deformed the relationship between humankind and God and how God, in his immense love and mercy, took the initiative to restore it for everyone who believes that God sent 'his Son to be the atoning sacrifice for our sins' (1 John 4:10).

However, the cry of dereliction was not the end of the drama. It was followed by three great cries of triumph. Two of them were uttered from

40

the cross: 'It is finished' (John 19:30) – the work of bearing the sin of the world and ending alienation was accomplished for all time; and, 'Father, into your hands I commend my spirit' (Luke 23:46) – reconciliation was complete. The third was announced by the angels at Jesus' tomb three days later: 'he is not here for he has been raised' (Matthew 28:6).

So, God's way of dealing with evil was to take upon himself the full force of every possible alienation. Jesus Christ submitted himself to being the scapegoat and the innocent lamb sacrificed in our place to free us from enmity towards God. The resurrection demonstrated that the power and consequences of sin had been broken and overcome. The outcome of this astonishing act was to make peace and reconciliation possible in all relationships.

The process of reconciliation

Reconciliation, then, has been made possible because of God's costly sacrifice. It can only happen, however, when alienated human beings are willing to make their own sacrifice by changing the direction of their lives. We can identify five steps that are necessary if a person wishes to enter into fellowship with God and in peace with their fellow human beings:

- Step 1 – *recognise* the abnormality of our lives, that we are part of a perverted world

- Step 2 – take *responsibility* for our personal share of bad thoughts and practices by admitting that we are guilty of wrongdoing

- Step 3 – *repent* of the contribution we have made to the deformity of human relationships and our rejection of God's love, justice and mercy. Repentance is much more than *regret* that things have gone wrong or *remorse* – that may be just a feeling of shame or self-reproach. Repentance is an act of the will – that is, a deliberate act of turning away from sin to the living God. It marks a decisive turning point in our lives;

- Step 4 – *receive* God's forgiveness and extend forgiveness to those who have wronged us and have sincerely said sorry

- Step 5 – make *restitution* for the offences and injustices we have committed (as Zacchaeus the tax collector did in the presence of Jesus – Luke 19:8)

The consequences of reconciliation

In the first place, we are *released* from guilt, hatred and bitterness both towards others (including God) and towards ourselves. In the New Testament, the verb to forgive (*aphiemi*) also means to liberate. In Luke 4: 18, for example, it could equally well be translated by either word. So, being assured of forgiveness for our opposition to God and our estrangement from other human beings, having repented, we are *rescued* from a guilty conscience and are at peace with our creator and his creation.

In the second place, we are *restored* to the wholeness of life. Thus, our enmity towards God and the acrimony and animosity we may feel towards others are transformed into friendships. We are *rid* of our disorientated lives.

Non-Christian responses to overcoming evil and promoting goodness

For the non-theist believer in the uncaring, impersonal process of natural selection without any purpose except the replication of the species, good and evil may be described and analysed, but it has no explanation. Those who deny the reality of our estrangement from the God who created us have never been able to give an adequate reason why hate is so often a more powerful emotion than love, or corruption more common than honesty. They are at a loss to know why people should choose to be violent towards others or defraud them of their goods, rather than be kind, generous and helpful towards them. Tzvetan Todorov, an atheist, humanist philosopher, in his book *The Imperfect Garden*, suggests the possibility that secularism could be viewed as one of the greatest contributors to evil, echoing the view that the origin of evil is to be found in the misuse of freedom.[1] Humans, he

---

[1] Tzvetan Todorov, *The Imperfect Garden: The Legacy of Humanism*

says, may have unwittingly accepted a kind of devil's pact (clearly echoing the story of Jesus' temptations by the devil) in which Satan offers them unlimited free will, meaning the power to choose exactly how they wish to live. However, Satan hides the cost of total autonomy, namely that it will destroy all relationships:

> If you want to keep your liberty ... you will have to pay a triple price, first by separating yourself from God, then from your neighbour and finally from yourself.

> No more God – you will be a 'materialist'. No more neighbour ... you will be an 'individualist' ... (No more self) ... you will be an alienated, inauthentic being.[2]

In the period between the end of the second World War and about 1990, existential philosophy was popular among certain classes of people. It described existence as absurd, drawing the conclusion that to embrace life was no more rational than to commit suicide. However, because it is impossible to construct one's life on the basis that everything is meaningless, existentialists rowed back from the realisation that, on their secular premises, all choices are arbitrary. Some proclaimed that humanity had now moved into a sphere of life beyond good and evil. However, they recoiled from the obvious conclusion to such a belief that, to take one example, caring for and nurturing a young child is no more commendable than doing it harm. Freedom to choose (the devil's seduction) is valueless, unless we know what is worthwhile to choose.

What about the devil's pact? According to Todorov, people react differently to the huge cost that is allegedly extracted from those who wish to enjoy an unbridled liberty:

- Some will say, as a matter of fact, that freedom is a mirage; it has never existed. We are deceived into believing that its attainment is a realistic goal. In fact, we are wholly determined by our genes, our upbringing and the way our brains work; all our responses are foreordained. We kid ourselves if we really believe we are free.

- Others will say, there is no devil to offer us the illusion of freedom in exchange for submission to his mastery. Let us, therefore, embrace

---

(Princeton, NJ: Princeton University Press, 2002).
2 Todorov, *The Imperfect Garden*, p. 3–4.

our liberation from these mythical scare stories, and do as we desire:

> Let man affirm himself in his essential solitude, in his freedom from all moral constraint ... Let him affirm his will to power, let him serve his own interests ... Instead of mourning, we should shout for joy.[3]

- Yet others, among whom Todorov counts himself, do not believe there ever was a pact with the devil. As humanists they believe that autonomy – the decision to obey no law, except those we prescribe for ourselves – does not necessarily entail any loss. There is no price to pay. Getting rid of God does not inevitably lead to loss of human community or one's identity and personality. The highest good is the right of individuals to be free from coercion, including the constraint and compulsion of following God's will.

These sentiments, in general, sum up the situation of Western culture at the present. It promotes and celebrates the supreme value of choice and, therefore, wages war against all restrictions on rights and liberties. The devil has enticed whole generations into believing, firstly, that the ends justify the means and, secondly, because we do not know what ends are valuable to select, to concentrate on the means. This is why, for so many, life is genuinely meaningless.

The humanist dilemma

In another book, *Memory as the Remedy for Evil*, Todorov asks the question: is it possible for good to eradicate evil by relentlessly bringing evil doers to justice?[4] Can we overcome evil by the power of memory, by contracting together to ensure that atrocities are never again committed? The answer he gives is a resounding 'no'! We cannot be delivered from evil. Memory has failed as a remedy against evil. He also stresses the fact that failure lies in our making too ready a distinction between the good and the bad, the victim and the villain.

He argues, therefore, against imposing excessive punishment on criminals and in favour of restorative justice. In other words, he appears

---

3 Todorov, *The Imperfect Garden*, p. 5.
4 Tzvetan Todorov, *Memory as the Remedy for Evil* (Chicago, MI: Seagull Books/University of Chicago Press, 2010).

to be saying that, because we cannot win the battle against evil, let us consider it less serious. If we are all evil, in one way or another, let us be less forceful in the way we treat criminals. However, there is a serious question about whether restorative justice is true justice. The attempt to persuade evil doers to change their habits is a wholly laudable enterprise. It should not, however, be equated with justice as such, but with the process of returning wrongdoers to society cured of their evil intents.

Justice recognises the severity of their anti-social behaviour by sentencing them to the punishment that their misconduct deserves. In other words, to act justly is to take with extreme gravity the serious nature of evil by penalising the perpetrator. At the same time, it is right to remember that no-one is exempt from the potential retribution of the law. To misunderstand the nature of evil seems to lead inevitably to a misapplication of the sanctions that justice requires.

In his first book, Todorov's remedy for evil consists in the practice of three essential values:

* the recognition of the equal dignity of all people

* altruism

* the basic freedom of all to act in ways that benefit their own interests, without harming those of others

On analysis, these three values amount to the promotion of self-interest. The values are all very high-sounding, but they are all designed to defend autonomous individuals against the arbitrary choices of others that might restrict their concerns. This is a morality that creates an effective barrier against the loss of freedom to be the person I choose to be.

In the secular humanist scheme of things, people are given no prescribed identity. There is no sense that human beings, by their very nature, are constituted in particular ways. Just as the universe and life is self-generated, so human beings are compelled by their secular beliefs to generate their own self – they become 'god' to themselves.

The atheist philosopher, A. C. Grayling, sees this as a problem, to which he has no solution. He considers the three main ideas of what makes human being tick that Sigmund Freud advances: *eros* (sexual desire),

Thanatos (the death wish) and destructive aggression.[5] For various reasons he rejects Freud's ideas, but he does not advance any possible alternatives. So, for him, human nature hangs in the air. As for Todorov, he supposes that freedom as autonomy seems the best way to define the human being.[6]

This is the best that the secular world can do as it creates modern and post-modern men and women. What, however, if we actually live in another kind of world, one that has been designed and constructed according to the eternal good pleasure of a God who is the very definition of the distinction between good and evil? What if we are obliged to live in this world, and all attempts to evade this and create our own universe result in frustration and disappointment? Surely, we would conclude that, by creating a world of our own choosing that denies the real world of God's choice, we have not struck a very satisfactory bargain for our lives.

Nevertheless, this is what secular humanists have chosen to do, and God respects their choice. At the same time, he condemns them to accept and live out the consequences of their choice. Grayling sums up his moral philosophy at the end of his book with these words:

> What is good? The answer can only be: 'The considered life – free, creative, informed and chosen, a life of achievement and fulfilment, of pleasure, understanding, love and friendship.'[7]

Is it too much to suggest that, tragically, his sentiments could be shared by someone dedicated to trafficking young girls for sexual exploitation? They could tick most, if not all, the elements that go into making up Grayling's 'considered life'.

So, the humanist finishes with the blatant lie that rejecting God's truth results in a higher concept of the human. To tell the real truth, flowing from conscience, the impact of God's law on Western culture, the ethic of Jesus and the example of the followers of Jesus, when true to his teaching, secular society still recognises the (ontological) reality of good and evil. However, being parasitic on Christian moral virtues, and having

---

5 A.C. Grayling, *What is Good? The Search for the Best Way to Live* (London: Weidenfield and Nicolson, 2003) p. 186.
6 Todorov, *Memory as the Remedy for Evil*, p. 47.
7 A. C. Grayling, *What is Good? The Search for the Best Way to Live* (London: Weidenfeld and Nicolson, 2003), p. 219.

no adequate foundation for its own, how long will a system of objective justice, built on rooting out all lies and corruption, last?

In this day and age of doubt, scepticism and ridicule, Christians still have a most powerful weapon – the truth about God, the universe and ourselves: God's truth. All other ideas, theories and beliefs have singularly failed, as they are bound to do. So, in all humility and gentleness, but with confidence and boldness, this is what we need to proclaim in the public square:

> *Jesus said, 'If you hold to my teaching, you are really my disciples. Then you will know the truth, and the truth will set you free. (John 8:31–32, NIV).*

Questions for reflection

1. How far do you think that overcoming alienation through reconciliation sums up the Christian understanding of the accomplishment of Christ's death and resurrection?
2. How would you explain the process of reconciliation to someone who enquires about the Christian faith?
3. To what extent do you think the so-called 'devil's pact' is an accurate way of describing the cause of sin and evil?
4. How would you describe the secular humanist's dilemma?

5. The Good Life: How Then Should we Live?

The humanist case for the good life

Humanism is a complete set of beliefs designed to explain the meaning of life in the vast universe. It is often used interchangeably with naturalism, atheism or some other form of non-theism. According to the website of the British Humanist Association, humanists believe that the good life can only be conducted in the absence of religious (or superstitious) beliefs.[1] Moral values follow from understanding human nature and interpreting experience in some way. Its convictions are based on reason, not on any supposed communication from some supernatural agency. It advocates a strong respect for others and for shared human values.

It considers that religious beliefs are both false and harmful and that, as a result, they hinder moral advancement. Humans, as far as we are currently aware, are alone in the universe. They are, therefore, accountable only to themselves for their choices. The greatest need is to learn to live without God. Charles Taylor in his massive exploration of the rise of secular societies sums up the humanist mood in the following way:

Conditions have arisen in the modern world in which it is no longer possible, honestly, rationally, without confusions, or fudging, or mental reservation, to believe in God. These conditions leave us nothing we can believe in beyond the human – human happiness or potentialities, or heroism.'[2]

---

[1] It is worth noting that the Christian faith would also claim to be humanist, but in an opposite sense to that being described here. It holds that its beliefs and moral values present the very best resources for genuine human flourishing, far outstripping what (secular) humanism offers. This is because it has a deeper understanding of how humans fit into the world as it is.

[2] Charles Taylor, *A Secular Age* (Cambridge, MA: Harvard University Press, 2007), p. 560.

The consequences and defects of the humanist perspective

If the universe is the result of impersonal forces that just happen to have produced life as we know it, then there are no guiding principles, intrinsic ends or rational processes that have at any stage shaped the various phases of life. Survival seems to be the only possible purpose built into a wholly mechanistic view of existence. On the basis of an impersonal beginning to the universe and life on earth, plus time plus chance, the human being is almost certainly a statistical impossibility.

Human beings can be explained up to a point by science in terms of their biological and mental attributes. However, their uninterrupted descent (or ascent?) from the higher primates is based on conjecture, not on evidence which is scientifically demonstrable. Such a surmise is the only theory that can be seriously considered as an alternative to divine creation. It is made necessary, not by good scientific evidence but by the non-scientific presumption that there is no God. Humanists have no answer to the question that humans, alone of all creatures, ask about the reason for existing, beyond the facile, superficial conclusion, 'that is the way it is'. To limit the explanation of all data to a strictly materialist interpretation of cause and effect makes a full understanding of the human being impossible.

If, for example, the impersonal forces of evolution are driven solely by the need to survive, we might ask how does an appreciation of beauty in the form of art further that end? Other living things – pigeons, for example – survive pretty well, without being able to enjoy the jazz classics of Duke Ellington, Dvorak's 'New World' symphony, the paintings of Rembrandt or Turner or the literature of Thomas Hardy or Dostoevsky.

Todorov's promotion of altruism as one of the basic elements of goodness might seem to be counterproductive to survival on a strictly naturalist interpretation of life. There does not appear to be any evolutionary advantage in sacrificing one's interests for those of another. If the great engine of evolution is survival, then it would be illogical to attempt to support and sustain the weakest members of the human species, rather than allow them to go to the wall. Thus, for example, it would be morally acceptable, indeed responsible, to abort all babies with congenital defects. Why spend huge sums of money on pre- and post-natal medical care

49

looking after them, when the gene pool will be amply replenished without them?

Scientific explanations of how the world is, valuable though they are, cannot possibly prescribe how humans ought to live. (In philosophy, the attempt to derive moral obligation from empirical data is called the 'naturalist fallacy'.) Observing nature alone, without any metaphysical preconceptions, is never going to produce a convincing rationale for defining the good, nor for explaining why it is our duty and responsibility to strive to lead a good life. Yet, somehow the humanist, relying on knowledge gained from science alone, is compelled to create ethical norms by breaking into the mechanist chain of biological determinism.

The most coherent humanist argument for moral values is provided by those who most consistently advance the naturalist evolutionary model. According to the evolutionary biologist, Michael Ruse, we are programmed to believe that co-operation is an obligation:

> Once we see that our moral beliefs are simply an adaptation put in place by natural selection, in order to further our reproductive ends, that is an end to it. Morality is no more than a collective illusion, fobbed off on us by our genes for reproductive ends.[1]

However, survival is not an objective built into evolution, for evolution has no objective. Survival is merely a description of what has happened to those species that are still with us today; in other words, it is a truism – something that has to be, given the circumstances. If everything is the result of chance, there is neither a biological nor moral necessity for anything to survive, or to evolve into the human species. If a colossal meteor were to hit the earth and extinguish all life on the planet, or if a nuclear winter were to descend on the world as the result of a nuclear catastrophe of huge proportions, these events would, on naturalistic evolutionary premises, be as equally morally valid as the continuation of life.

If the universe is wholly impersonal, then morality is entirely absent; an evolutionary process is totally indifferent to the issue of survival or extinction. If, by some extraordinary miracle, human beings have evolved

---

[1] Michael Ruse, 'The Significance of Evolution' in Peter Stringer (ed.), *A Companion to Ethics* (Oxford: Blackwell, 1993), p. 506.

out of a pitiless, detached, amoral process, but with a sense of right and wrong, on a naturalist reading of existence this is no more than a cruel joke. If naturalism is true, it does not make sense. As far as science is concerned, there is no moral obligation to survive; this is a value assumed entirely on other, non-scientific, grounds.

Human rights as the basis for the good life

At the end of the last chapter, we stated that the moral sensibilities of the humanist are parasitic on the ethical values of the Christian faith. Even if God does not exist and, therefore, moral absolutes do not exist, it is still highly beneficial to human life to believe that they do. An ethicist, John Mackie, known for his atheistic views, states that 'morality works because of human beings overwhelming propensity to believe in right and wrong.'[2] However, this view creates two huge problems for the atheist.

Firstly, if the evolutionary process is completely devoid of any moral scruples, how does one account for this apparently inborn propensity to believe in right and wrong? Clearly it is an added-on extra introduced from outside the process, not part of it.

Secondly, it is tantamount to saying that morality is based on a *deception* (like believing in Father Christmas or fairies at the bottom of the garden) or an *illusion*.[3] If morality is only a useful instrument, on pragmatic grounds, for tricking us into believing that the distinction between right and wrong is categorical, why not call the bluff? The criminal could then defend his activities by saying that the law, which he has broken, only reflects an arbitrary morality hoisted onto the common person by those who have appropriated power to themselves. He is, therefore, just as entitled to his own equally subjective version. At one time, radical socialists used to hold this view with reference to bourgeois morality.

In order to attempt to evade this dilemma, our contemporary, secular societies have taken over the notion of human rights as a foundation for formulating the good life. They are presented as a way of filling a moral vacuum. The notion seems to have become a kind of substitute for God:

---

[2]   J. L. Mackie, *Ethics: Inventing Right and Wrong* (Harmondsworth: Penguin Books, 1977), p. 43.

[3]   Incidentally, one cannot but help suggesting that Ruse is a very apt surname for one who holds his views about the origin of moral values.

51

they have become omnipresent, unqualified, unquestionable, often arbitrary and absurd. (One of the latest far-fetched claims – and they are increasing in number and ingenuity the whole time – is the right of parents to take their children out of school during term-time, in the belief that a family is owed a cheaper holiday than is possible during school holiday times. If this alleged right became applied universally, education of the young would descend into chaos).

What are rights?

A right is supposedly an entitlement to something that is intrinsically good, which I am owed on the basis either of who I am, what I do or what I possess. A right assumes an agent whose responsibility it is to see that the entitlement is granted. The responsibility, presumably, lies with bodies that frame laws concerning rights and those that oversee their implementation. However, this notion of rights is close to arguing in a circle: a responsibility corresponds to a right (which is assumed), and if such an entity as a right exists, then naturally it entails a responsibility.

This argument begs the initial question: why does anyone have to recognise another person's postulated rights. From where does the notion of rights come? According to the *American Declaration of Independence* (July 4, 1776[4]), it seems to emanate from God. It declares, first, that 'it is a self-evident truth that all are created equal'. However, secondly, it affirms that rights are an endowment from the creator. In the version adopted by *The Universal Declaration of Human Rights*, still the template for all subsequent Declarations or Conventions, the word creator drops out.[5] Article 1 of the Universal Declaration of Human Rights says, 'All human beings are born free and equal in dignity and rights. They are endowed with reason and conscience'. Presumably the mention of a creator is deemed unacceptable either to secularists or to non-theistic religions. The Declaration does not specify the source of rights. It simply declares their existence as a manifest fact; it is as if it were affirming that human beings are born into the world possessing two eyes, two ears, a nose, a mouth and equal human rights. That all are born free and with

---

[4] https://www.archives.gov/founding-docs/declaration-transcript

[5] United Nations, *Universal Declaration of Human Rights*, Paris, 1948, https://www.un.org/en/universal-declaration-human-rights/index.html

equal dignity is historically untrue. Two hundred years ago, slavery was accepted by societies as a natural condition, decided by the lottery of birth. Slavery, in one form or another, is still common in most nations today.

Do rights exist?

The language of rights arose in modern, secular usage along with the social creation of the autonomous, individual, moral agent. It has become a dogma, without any basis in science or reason. Empirically, there is much evidence against the idea. It assumes the essential and equal dignity and value of all human beings, without exception or qualification. However, where human beings clearly are not equal – either physically, intellectually or in terms of the circumstances of their birth – why should not those endowed with greater abilities, attributes, skills and power, use them to their advantage? What is a sufficient basis for considering other people's interests equal to or more insistent than ours? These questions can hardly be answered on the basis of our alleged evolutionary past. George Orwell's famous saying, 'all animals are equal but some animals are more equal than others' can be paralleled by another saying, 'all things that survive are equal, but some things survive in a more favourable way than others'.[6]

The reality is that the intrinsic dignity and worth (sacredness) of human beings can only be inferred from a status that is conferred on them from outside the natural order. It would seem that, in comparison with all conceivable alternatives, only the biblical concept of the *imago Dei* can give a sufficient grounding. Only in the existence of an entirely good and wise supreme creator, in whose likeness human beings are made, can come the conviction that they should be protected from exploitation.

Human life is, first and foremost, a gift from God. Therefore, it is to be protected from all those who seek to deny the gift by rejecting the equality, value and freedoms of all, decreed by the creator. As one non-Christian has recognised,

Rights are conclusions [arrived at by] long chains of reasoning

---

[6] George Orwell, *Animal Farm* (Harmondsworth: Penguin Books, 2008), Chapter 10.

based on core beliefs; they are not foundations.[7]

So, as far as moral principles are concerned, the secular humanist tries to substitute self-evident, irrefutable, basic rights in the place of a morally perfect God who has shown us the only way to live in accordance with his exemplary will. It cannot be done. The emperor has lost his clothes. Or, to change the metaphor, while people were not looking closely enough to detect the trick, the rabbit has been pulled from the hat!

God's provision for a good life

From a Christian perspective, everything stems from God's act of reconciliation. Only those who respond positively to the good news that Christ's one act of bearing away the guilt of our failings has supplied the full solution to the problem of the abuse of freedom, can begin a new life (2 Corinthians 5:17). This new creation is the key to Christian teaching on ethics. The believer dwells in Christ and the Spirit of Jesus dwells in the believer. Transformation happens from the inside out.

The Sermon on the Mount

When thinking of a Christian-inspired moral life, people often turn to the Sermon on the Mount (Matthew 5–7). It is said by many to represent the highest pattern of virtuous living. The beatitudes ('Blessed are you...'), for example, have been interpreted as a kind of general, universal transaction or contract between human beings: 'do x and you will receive y, and this will be a blessing for you.'

However, it is not the intention of the Beatitudes to exhort people to follow a certain type of behaviour. Rather, they make a statement about the reality of a new life: the kind of people, who are part of God's new creation will be 'poor in spirit', 'humble', 'merciful', 'pure in heart', 'peace makers,' and so on. The Beatitudes affirm a spirituality already implanted in the person who accepts the salvation offered through Jesus Christ. They should, therefore, be read in the following way: look at the joyfulness of people who already possess, or will possess x, not as a reward but as a free gift of God's grace working in the life of the believer. Transformation

---

7 John Gray, *The Two Faces of Liberalism* (Cambridge: Polity Press, 2000), p. 84–85; my emphasis.

is not achieved by following a system of law or living by a set of values in our own strength, but by the supernatural work of the triune God, growing in the believer as the fruit of the Spirit.

When the apostle Paul reminds Gentile converts of the kind of life required of followers of Jesus, he tells them about the truth as it is in Jesus and instructs them to get a new 'wardrobe of clothes' (Ephesians 4:20–24; Colossians 3:9–11), freely offered by God. The new clothes equate to the fruit of the Spirit, active in the life of those who trust in Christ (Galatians 5:22–25). The reality of life is that disorders come from within the will and affections of humans (Mark 7:15). Often, they are the result of the way we react to temptations, pressures and adverse circumstances. As examples of new life in Christ, we can follow Paul's list in Romans 12:17–21. These are not so much imperatives, as indicatives. They express the new life that flows from the new birth.

The Christian community is called to be a model and agent of reconciliation. Nothing damages a witness to the power of Jesus to bring about change more than unresolved conflicts within the Church. Reconciliation involves at least the following elements:

- *Practising justice.* Sometimes the church will be called on to exercise discipline, when a member or members have behaved in ways that bring reproach upon the community. It will operate discipline in a way that can be seen to be absolutely fair, making sure that the facts of the case are clear, that those accused have an opportunity to defend themselves and, if found guilty, to repent. They should not be humiliated or made to feel resentment. The purpose of discipline is not to punish people for the sake of it, but to restore them completely to the fellowship (Matthew 18:15–17; Galatians 6:1; James 5:19–20). Separating a brother or sister from the fellowship is a last resort, when all other attempts to bring about reconciliation and restore peace have failed.

- *Eliminating discrimination based on the circumstances of our birth.* Diversity is enriching for a community when it is part of the normative variety of creation in races, ethnic groups, cultures, nationalities, gender or age. It is also to be accepted, even when caused by external factors as, for example, in the case of disability or poverty. In the latter two cases, however, diversity should also be treated as abnormal, and therefore be the object of change.

55

- *Pursuing forgiveness in the place of condemnation and a judgemental attitude.* Condemnation expects perfection, when all faults and mistakes are eliminated. It may come from a desire to go on finding fault and laying blame. It does not expect, from the other an attitude of sorrow and a determination to make amends. An over harsh denunciation of others may arise from disappointment. It may reflect our own shadow side, when we hope that criticism of our failings will be deflected on to another, and our lives in comparison will be made to look benign. In contrast, the true Christian attitude is to long for a person's forgiveness and restoration to wholeness: 'there is more joy in heaven over one sinner who repents' (Luke 15: 7, 10). And we are all sinners; all under the same judgement. We will be judged by the way we judge others (Romans 2:1–2).

- *Banishing all notions of vengeance and retaliation,* even when provoked by violence and justified anger. Evil cannot be overcome by perpetrating further evil, only by doing good (Romans 12:19–21). In the case of the legitimate use of force to restrain violent people, as the lesser of two evils, or the punishment of those guilty of criminal behaviour, justice is served only when retribution is carefully controlled by independent agents.

- *Exercising power in new ways.* Power is not in itself corrupt or corrupting. Nevertheless, because it has a tendency in this direction, individuals and society as a whole need to be eternally vigilant. Power must always be accountable democratically – that is, through corporate, open, non-coercive, decision-making structures and processes, especially in the church. The right use of authority depends on its being always open to correction, being a shared responsibility, not insisting on its own way and being impartial.

All in all, nothing demonstrates more clearly the reality of God's power at work, the truth of the good news concerning Jesus and authentic renewal in the Spirit than genuine reconciliation.

Questions for reflection

1. Charles Taylor talks about 'conditions' that exist in the modern world that make belief in God for many no longer possible. What, in your opinion, are these conditions?

2. Why is a true understanding of the good life so hard for those who believe that human existence is the result of pure chance?

3. The demand to have individual rights implemented has grown rapidly in recent years. What are the problems that have arisen as a result?

4. Why is the gift of new life the key to Christian ethical practice?

Postscript

In these five chapters, I have attempted to show how Christian convictions about the crucial issues of life are entirely rational, how they provide the best explanation for the meaning of human existence, how they can be lived consistently, and why alternative accounts of life and answers to fundamental questions are inadequate. Here we have, I believe, powerful reasons for being able to persuade non-Christians of the truth of Christian belief and practices – by demonstrating that it gives the most satisfactory answers to questions about the origin of all existence and life, human identity, the nature of evil and how it may be overcome and how the good life, the restoration of human beings' full humanity to what the creator intends, may be achieved. Having said all we have, in favour of recognising and submitting ourselves to the truth, there is nothing more persuasive, more likely to convince sceptics that they need God to remake their lives, than a living demonstration of a life made new by the grace of God.

A robust intellectual advocacy of Christian faith in a world which is largely ignorant of what it stands for and why is an indispensable part of Christian witness. We have seen how convincing its answers to the most basic problems of human living are, because it is able to penetrate to their root causes, whether of an individual or social nature. We have also perceived how weak the alternative views of secular humanists are, when challenged by the same questions.[1] At the same time, there is no greater advocacy of the truth of the Christian message than a life transformed by the action of God. A living witness that demonstrates the reality on the ground of all that Christians claim in their verbal communication of the good news about Jesus Christ is a powerful confirmation that here is a belief that stands up to the test of practical living.

---

[1] It would also be possible to show the inability of the world's major religions to explain fully the nature of reality. This would require a separate study. I have attempted to address this issue in a book, written nearly thirty years ago, but I think still trustworthy in its arguments: J. Andrew Kirk, *Loosing the Chains: Religion as opium and liberation* (London: Hodder and Stoughton, 1992).

In Western secular societies, there are many strident voices that paint the Christian faith in almost wholly negative terms. They choose to highlight only those historical episodes where people, bearing the name of Christian, have denied by their actions the faith they claim to profess. They deliberately ignore, however, the countless stories of Christians unassumingly dedicating their lives to eradicating diseases, caring for the sick and disabled, protecting vulnerable children, initiating job-promoting schemes in areas of high unemployment, campaigning for justice against exploitation and corruption, providing education and training where they do not exist, and so on and so forth; the list is almost limitless.

Naturally, Christians never claim that they have or can solve all problems, given the hardness of people's hearts. Even less do they pretend that they are faultless, for it is a central part of the Christian message that in God's mercy and forgiveness, there is always a way back from failure. They are, despite a common assumption to the contrary, well aware of the dangers of hypocrisy, spiritual pride and moralistic judgementalism. All of these are firmly and frequently condemned in the teaching of their Scriptures.

So, in the final analysis, Christians affirm that in God's action in the world, in creation and in reconciliation, they have been enabled to perceive totally adequate rational, spiritual and moral answers to the persistent troubles and dilemmas that face every generation. These form the basis of an enduring hope that can be offered to a world that so desperately needs it:

> *Always be prepared to give an answer to everyone who asks you to give the reason for the hope that you have ... Do this with gentleness and respect. (1 Peter 3:15, NIV)*

Question for reflection

What is the most significant idea that you will take away from this book?

Further reading

William Lane Craig and Chad Meister (eds.), *God is Great, God is Good: Why Believing in God is Reasonable and Responsible* (Downers Grove, IL: IVP Books, 2009)

Douglas Groothuis, *Christian Apologetics: A Comprehensive Case for Biblical Faith* (Downers Grove, IL: IVP Academic, 2011)

J. Andrew Kirk, *The Future of Reason, Science and Faith: Following Modernity and Post-Modernity* (Andover: Ashgate Press, 2007)

J. Andrew Kirk, *Being Human: An Historical Inquiry Into Who We Are* (Eugene, OR: Wipf and Stock, 2019)

John C. Lennox, *God's Undertaker: Has Science Buried God?* (Oxford: Lion Hudson, 2009)

Alister McGrath, *The Twilight of Atheism: The Rise and Fall of Disbelief in the Modern World* (London: Doubleday, 2004)

Alister McGrath, *Dawkins' God: Genes, Memes and the Meaning of Life* (Oxford: Blackwell Publishing, 2005)

Richard Milton, *Shattering the Myths of Darwinism* (Rochester, VM: Park Street Press, 1997)

Recently Released by the Latimer Trust

What does the Bible really say? Addressing Revisionist Arguments on Sexuality and the Bible *by Martin Davie*

In 2019 a series of ten articles by various authors was published on the liberal Anglican website ViaMedia.News under the collective title 'Does the Bible Really Say....?' The purpose of this series was to challenge the belief that the Bible rules out acceptance of same-sex sexual relationships and same-sex marriage.

The essays in this book are response to these ViaMedia. News articles. They show that the arguments that these articles put forward are not sustainable in the light of what the Bible actually says. Underlying the current debate in the Church about human sexuality is the question asked of Eve by the snake 'Did God really say?' (Genesis 3:1). Through nature and Scripture God has said clearly that he has created human beings as male and female and has ordained marriage between one man and one woman as the sole legitimate setting for sexual intercourse. We know that this is what God has told us and yet in the face of pressure from our contemporary culture we are tempted to question whether this is what he really meant. It is of the utmost importance that this temptation is resisted. The purpose of this book is to encourage such resistance.

'Doubt not...but Earnestly Believe' A Fresh Look at the BCP Baptist Service *by Mark Pickles*

While Common Worship (2000) provides a Book of Common Prayer Communion (BCP) in modern English, sadly there is no such provision for the BCP baptism service. For some Anglican evangelicals this may not seem to be a particularly regrettable omission.

There are those who might not be persuaded of the biblical mandate for baptising infants, whilst others might have concerns over some of the language used that may appear to affirm 'baptismal regeneration'. This booklet is an attempt not only to engage with those questions and concerns but also to proffer an enthusiastic support for the theology and liturgical content of the BCP Baptism service. It has a great emphasis on the covenantal grace of God which encourages Christian parents to "doubt not – but earnestly believe" in God's faithfulness and mercy. In so doing it directs our primary focus to our promise keeping God and not to ourselves.

OTHER RECOMMENDATIONS

Thomas Cranmer: Using the Bible to Evangelize the Nation *by Peter Adam*

We need not only to do evangelism, but also develop contemporary gospel strategies which we trust, under God, will be effective. We need gospel wisdom, as well as gospel work. We need to work on local evangelism, but also work on God's global gospel plan. This alerts us to our own nation, as well as other nations. Gospel strategy includes the question, 'How should we evangelise our nation?' Thomas Cranmer, Archbishop of Canterbury 1532-56, strategised and worked to do this from the perspective of Anglican Reformed theology and practice. We cannot duplicate his plan in detail, but he can inspire us, and also teach us the key ingredients of such a plan.

His context of ministry had advantages and disadvantages! Our context has the same mixture. We can also learn from Cranmer's ability to work effectively in his context, despite the many problems, and the suffering he endured. God used him to evangelise his nation at his time. May God use us for his gospel glory!